August 2010

Viv & Nick,

Here are some Montreal memories
for you to take with you on your new
adventure . . . .

with our love and best wishes

Kim, David and the Redpath Clan !!

MONTRÉAL

Technical Notes
Most of the photographs in this book were taken with a Pentax 67 camera using a 35-mm fisheye lens,
45-mm and 75-mm wide-angle lenses, a standard 105-mm lens, and 165-mm and 300-mm telephoto lenses.
A few photographs were produced using a Horseman 4" x 5" large-format camera with 75-mm, 90-mm and 210-mm lenses.
On rare occasions a 35-mm Nikon camera was used. All shots were captured on Fujichrome film.
Although filters were used for many of the shots, none of the images in this book
has been altered by computer in order to heighten visual impact.

Cover Photo: Yves Marcoux/Publiphoto

This book was produced using the Éditions de l'Homme laser imaging system, which includes:

Apple Inc. computers

An Intergraph server distributed by Aldin Graphics Inc.

A Scitex Smart ' 720 digitalizer

An RIP 50 PL2 image processor combined with the latest Lino Dot®, Lino Pipeline® and Linotype-Hell® technology.

Cataloguing in Publication Data (Canada)

Marcoux, Yves
    Montréal: The Lights of My City
    Translation of Montréal: les lumières de ma ville

    1. Montréal (Québec) – Pictorial works
    I. Pharand, Jacques. II. Title.

FC2947.37.M37   1999   971.4'28'00222   C99-941325-2
F1054.5.M843M37   1999

The publisher gratefully acknowledges the support of the Société de développement des entreprises culturelles du Québec for its publishing program.

We gratefully acknowledge the support of the Canada Council for the Arts for its publishing program.

We acknowledge the financial support of the Government of Canada through the Book Publishing Industry Development Program (BPIDP) for our publishing activities.

© 2000, Les Éditions de l'Homme,
a division of the Sogides Group

Legal deposit: Fourth quarter 2000
Bibliothèque nationale du Québec

ISBN 2-7619-1558-5

EXCLUSIVE DISTRIBUTORS:

· For Canada and the USA:
MESSAGERIES ADP*
955 Amherst St.
Montréal, Quebec
H2L 3K4
Tel.: (514) 523-1182
Fax: (514) 939-0406
* A subsidiary of Sogides Ltée

· For France and other countries:
INTER FORUM
Immeuble Paryseine, 3, Allée de la Seine
94854 Ivry Cedex
Tel.: 01 49 59 11 89/91
Fax: 01 49 59 11 96
Orders: Tel.: 02 38 32 71 00
        Fax: 02 38 32 71 28

· For Switzerland:
DIFFUSION: HAVAS SERVICES SUISSE
Case postale 69 - 1701 Fribourg, Switzerland
Tel.: (41-26) 460-80-60
Fax: (41-26) 460-80-68
Internet: www.havas.ch
E-mail: office@havas.ch
DISTRIBUTION: OLF SA
Z.I. 3, Corminbœuf
P.O. Box 1061
CH-1701 FRIBOURG
Orders: Tel.: (41-26) 467-53-33
        Fax: (41-26) 467-54-66

· For Belgium and Luxembourg:
PRESSES DE BELGIQUE S.A.
Boulevard de l'Europe 117
B-1301 Wavre
Tel.: (010) 42-03-20
Fax: (010) 41-20-24

For more information about publications, please visit our website: **www.edhomme.com**
Other sites of interest: www.edjour.com
www.edtypo.com · www.edvlb.com
www.edhexagone.com · www.edutilis.com

MONTRÉAL

The Lights of My City

Photos : YVES MARCOUX
Text : Jacques Pharand

LES ÉDITIONS DE L'HOMME

To my father.
In memory of my mother.
From them, I learned perseverance and gained the ability to appreciate the true value of
one of the most beautiful gifts I received at birth, the gift of sight.

Acknowledgements

Thanks to the team at Boréalis Photo Lab Inc. for their top quality work and for their financial support.

Special thanks to my colleagues and friends Marc-André Côté and Jean-Marc Petit,
who encouraged, supported and enlightened me with their priceless advice.

Thanks to the team at the Tony Stone Images photolibrary and to Michel Faugère at Publiphoto
for their confidence in me.

Finally, my affectionate thanks to Lucie, my spouse, who allowed me to live out my passion.
Her generosity gave me the opportunity to fulfill one of my most cherished dreams — that of publishing this album.

Western downtown as seen from Île Notre-Dame.
Despite appearances, none of the buildings is higher than the cross on Mount Royal (visible at right) (pages 6-7).

The magnificent French pavilion built for the 1967 World's Fair
is now home to the Casino de Montréal (page 8).

Designed by Roger Taillibert, the world's tallest inclined tower overshadows
the stadium built for the Olympic Games of 1976 (pages 10-11).

Montréal's downtown and South Shore as seen from the Mount Royal chalet (pages 12-13).

A new generation of buildings north of Sainte-Catherine Street testifies
to Montréal's continuing evolution (pages 14-15).

Introduction

Just as clay in a potter's hands is gradually shaped into a magnificent vase, the humble village of Ville-Marie has gradually evolved into the harmonious city we know today. But how well do we really know Montréal?

Montrealers bustle about with their own active lives in the midst of a city itself in perpetual motion, rarely stopping to appreciate the particular qualities, the distinctive details, that make up the vast masterpiece that is Montréal. The pictures in this book, however, compel us to stop and take a fresh look at familiar sights in a different light and from a unique perspective.

We hope this collection reflects the charms of a city where the past blends with the future, where each neighbourhood expresses its unique personality, and where the delicate interplay between nature and architecture is there for all to enjoy. May you discover in these pages the too-often unappreciated sights of a one-of-a-kind city as seen through the eyes of an admiring photographer. A gourmet feast of light and colour, just waiting for you to dig in . . .

A heavy snowfall blankets Drolet Street,
a stone's throw from Square Saint-Louis.

Montréal, an island

You will, no doubt, be surprised to learn that Montréal is but the largest of some one hundred islands making up the Montréal archipelago, its geographical designation. Many are still pretty much as Jacques Cartier found them in 1534. Others, however, were soon settled and are today satellites of the metropolis. So, in fact, we will be talking about not one, but several islands.

There was an obvious military advantage associated with the island of Montréal in the colony's early years — its location downstream from the Lachine Rapids made it almost impregnable. However, Montréal never was a target of devastating attacks and progressed on the commercial front unhampered by armed conflict and its aftermath.

History tells us that fewer than twenty years after the founding of Ville-Marie by Paul Chomedey, Sieur de Maisonneuve, in 1642, François Le Ber obtained the fief of Île Saint-Paul. The island was acquired by the Sisters of the Congregation of Notre-Dame in 1720 and has been known ever since as Île des Sœurs (Nun's Island). In 1677, a second island of the archipelago was given away, this time to Commanding Officer Jacques Bizard, an aide-de-camp

Tourist excursion boats anchored in the Clock Tower Basin, near the Bonsecours Market (page 18).

The Parc Jean-Drapeau (foreground) is linked to the metropolis by the Jacques Cartier Bridge.

to Governor Frontenac during his first term, as a reward for his services. This island is still known as Île Bizard.

Early in the 18th century, Île Branchereau in the Rivière des Prairies was developed by the Sulpicians, who built a bridge linking it to Montréal island in 1726. The island became known as Île de la Visitation when the Montréal parish of La-Visitation-de-la-Bienheureuse-Vierge-Marie was established in 1736.

Rather than recount every subsequent addition of smaller islands to Montréal, we will limit ourselves to one last, pertinent example — Île Sainte-Hélène.

Named by Samuel de Champlain in 1611 in honour of his wife, Hélène Boulé, Île Sainte-Hélène was given to Charles Le Moyne, the first lord of Longueuil, in 1665. On

September 7, 1760, knight François-Gaston de Lévis burned his flags on this site, following the surrender of Montréal by then-Governor Pierre de Vaudreuil. Ceded back to the government in 1818, the island proved an irresistible attraction for Montrealers, although they had to ferry across the St. Lawrence in order to picnic there.

Bought by the city in 1907, Île Sainte-Hélène became more accessible only in 1930 when the Harbour Bridge — renamed the Jacques Cartier Bridge in 1934 — served to link Montréal to south shore Longueuil. A bus service was soon inaugurated, and Montrealers adopted Île Sainte-Hélène as a favourite summer destination.

Île Sainte-Hélène's biggest moment was in 1965 when the island was connected with its neighbours, the Ronde, Verte and Moffat islands, and the artificial Île Notre-Dame. These four islands together formed Parc-des-Îles, renamed Parc Jean-Drapeau in

The steeples of de la Visitation church as seen from the island bearing the same name.

honour of Montréal's famous mayor. In 1967,
Parc-des-Îles was home to the 1967 World's Fair,
"Man and His World." Since then, a metro sta-
tion has provided year-round service to the site.

Whoever mentions the word "island" will
— sooner or later — mention bridges, for what
begins as a settlement's military advantage soon
becomes its Achilles heel. To counter insular se-
clusion, a drawback to communications and
commerce, Montréal soon erected bridges, linking it both to the neighbouring islands and to
the continent.

The first ferryboat connecting Montréal
with Île Jésus (now the city of Laval) since 1801 was replaced in 1834 with a covered
wooden bridge built by the miller François Persilier, nicknamed Lachapelle. In 1859, a
second bridge was built across the Rivière des Prairies, this time from the village of Back
River, now known as the Ahuntsic district. With the arrival of railroads in 1836 came the
construction of the first railway bridge at Sainte-Anne-de-Bellevue, in 1854. It was soon
followed by the Victoria Tubular Bridge, the first across the St. Lawrence River, completed on December 17, 1859. This 2.27-km-long masterpiece was rebuilt on its same foot-
ings forty years later in order to accommodate trains, pedestrians and automobiles. The
construction of the St. Lawrence Seaway in 1959 required a daring solution — an alternate structure that would circumvent the St. Lambert locks at the bridge's south end,
thus avoiding interruptions caused by maritime traffic.

The advent of the automobile era generated the need for additional bridges; the
Jacques Cartier Bridge was the first specifically intended for car traffic. Thereafter,
Montréal added other bridges, noteworthy for different reasons: the Honoré-Mercier
Bridge supported the first high-voltage power lines feeding the city; the amazing
orthotropic span of the Papineau-Leblanc Bridge to Laval with its daring design; and

The weir of the hydroelectric station on the Rivière des Prairies
at the eastern tip of Île de la Visitation.

the Champlain Bridge, completed in 1965, at 6.5 km the longest St. Lawrence crossing. Finally, the Louis Hippolyte Lafontaine Tunnel, 1.4 km of sections in assembled dry dock, was a masterpiece of engineering craftsmanship.

Whatever the season, Montréal's eighteen bridges are perfect subjects for photographers. In the following pages, as you see them from new and unusual perspectives, you will, no doubt, marvel at the geometric grandeur of these works of art spanning impressive waterways.

The Victoria Bridge's alternate deck allows for its uninterrupted
use despite maritime traffic in the seaway.

The Clock Tower Basin as seen
from Île Sainte-Hélène.

The Concorde Bridge provides access to Île Notre-Dame
and the Casino de Montréal (foreground)
from the Bickerdike Pier.

A shuttle craft getting ready for mooring
at the Jacques Cartier berth.

One ship transfers its container cargo
while another sails in the harbour channel past
the petroleum refineries in Montréal-Est.

Ice floes on the St. Lawrence
do not hamper the operations
of the Port of Montréal.

In a Dantesque scene, most of the downtown core is obscured
by a -35°C dry fog rising from the St. Lawrence.

Rush-hour traffic on the Jacques Cartier Bridge (page 28).

Held up by its elegant middle towers alone, the Papineau-Leblanc Bridge
rests on the tip of Île de la Visitation before crossing the Rivière des Prairies (page 29).

Despite the eddies of the Sainte-Marie current, the St. Lawrence appears deceptively
motionless against the background of downtown (pages 30-31).

Pleasure crafts moored at the Old Port marina at the foot of Place Jacques-Cartier (page 32).

Harbour-cruise boats await excursionists in the Clock Tower Basin.

Seen from the South Shore, the steel arches of
the Champlain Bridge spanning the St. Lawrence Seaway
frame the buildings of the downtown core.

A bird's-eye view of the Papineau-Leblanc Bridge
and Île de la Visitation.

Aerial view of the Victoria Bridge with Île des Sœurs
(Nun's Island) and the piles of the Champlain Bridge
in the background.

The Jacques Cartier Bridge and the rides of La Ronde from the Clock Tower promenade.

The Clock Tower and its elegant promenade mark the access to Montréal's Old Port (page 37).

Its elegance alive with light, the Jacques Cartier
Bridge links Île Sainte-Hélène (right) to
Montréal's east end.

The St. Lawrence River cuts a swath between the downtown area of the metropolis and the suburbs of the South Shore.

On a winter morning, a solitary stroller contemplates the southwest area of Montréal from the Mount Royal chalet.
The Champlain Bridge is visible, at right (pages 40-41).

The raised central arch of the Champlain
Bridge provides clearance for ships travelling
along the St. Lawrence Seaway.

Beyond the mist rising
from the St. Lawrence,
downtown Montréal on
a pleasant winter afternoon.

Montréal, a city of history

Of all the North American cities, Montréal's historic old city undoubtedly has the most interesting legacy. Barely one kilometre square, Old Montréal is bounded by the St. Lawrence River, McGill and Berri streets and by what was once a natural barrier, little St. Martin River, where the Ville-Marie Expressway is now located.

An observant explorer can identify without difficulty the four distinct sections of the rapidly growing city. The eastern portion is primarily residential, while commercial activity is concentrated in the western counterpart. The thriving financial sector has grown up along Saint-Jacques Street, while administrative buildings fill the northern area.

If the city can pride itself on its historical heritage, it is thanks to the collective efforts of many artisans. The first was most certainly François Dollier de Casson, head of the Sulpicians, to whom was awarded the seigneury of Montréal in 1663. Not only did he undertake in 1680 the digging of the Lachine Canal, by-passing the rapids on the St. Lawrence and completed in 1825, but he also requested land surveyor Bénigne Bas-set to outline the first land-registry survey plan of the city. And in 1716, Gédéon de Catalogne and Gaspard Chaussegros de Léry replaced the early palisades with sturdy, permanent fortifications, the population having quadrupled in the preceding fifty years.

Rebuilt in 1926, Montreal's City Hall has retained the refinements of its original Second Empire features (page 44).

The Nelson Column towers above Place Jacques-Cartier.

But the least known of historically significant events is probably the role of administrator Claude Thomas Dupuy, who, in an edict dated June 17, 1727, issued the city's first building code; it required, for example, the alignment of building facades, masonry construction, the installation of firewalls and fireproof floors and the use of non-combustible roofing materials. In any case, major fires in 1721, 1734 and 1754 destroyed most of the earlier wood buildings, which had been erected in a more or less anarchical fashion.

A second change happened early in the 19th century — the fortifications were torn down to make way for the inevitable expansion of the city. One of the chief craftsmen of

this era was unquestionably John Ostell, architect, engineer and land surveyor. After the opening of the Lachine Canal, he was entrusted with the construction of the first Customs building on Place Royale in 1838 and then that of the old court-house in 1851. As the diocese's designated architect, Ostell was also responsible for the construction of the steeples of Notre-Dame Basilica in 1841, those of St. Ann and Notre-Dame-de-Grâce churches, and the enlargement of de la Visitation church.

And, of course, Montréal would not be Montréal without its public markets. After fire destroyed St. Raphaël College in 1803, it was decided not to rebuild it but to convert the site into a public place instead. Thus the market at Place Jacques-Cartier was created, merging its operations with those of justice, as a pillory was in use there until 1841.

The cupola of the Bonsecours Market rests
on a circle of doric columns.

Soon after being incorporated in 1831, Montréal equipped itself with a multi-purpose building that housed administrative offices, reception halls and a public market. Inspired by Boston's Quincy Market, built in 1826, the building's architect, William Footner, proved his originality by giving the Bonsecours Market two facades, one on Saint-Paul Street and another on de la Commune Street. The cupola crowning the building was the work of architect George Browne. Completed in 1846, the Bonsecours Market was used as city hall from 1852 to 1873 and was also briefly used as United Canada's parliament, after the destruction of its previous location in 1849.

But the history of Montréal is more than an inventory of buildings. Many monuments recall persons and events mark-ing its evolution. Thus as early as 1765, a bust of King George III stood in Place d'Armes. In Decem-ber 1805, the announce-ment of Admiral Horatio Nelson's death, after win-ning the Battle of Trafal-gar, stirred public senti-ment so much that a public fundraising cam-paign was immediately launched to finance construction of a monu-ment to his memory. On August 17, 1809, con-struction of the majestic Nelson Column was begun. It was eventually topped with a statue of the admiral, who, oddly enough, has his back turned to the river.

At times, popular enthusiasm generated a plethora of testimonials marking meaningful events. Thus a monument, a statue and a cross in different locations in the Ahuntsic area all recall the death-by-drowning of Father Nicolas Viel, a Récollet missionary, on June 25, 1625. Likewise, the city has sometimes multiplied its expressions of gratitude by erecting memorials and naming landmarks. For example, the memory of Queen Victoria is preserved with no less than a bust, a statue, two streets, a bridge and a square.

The western edge of Windsor Station, which opened to railway traffic in 1889.

Strollers walking the streets of the city will have no problem identifying the heroes who played a significant role in Montréal's history. From Maisonneuve to Dollard des Ormeaux, from Jeanne Mance to Marguerite Bourgeoys, from Pierre Le Moyne d'Iberville to George-Étienne Cartier, from the Patriots to those who fought in the Boer War, Montréal remembers.

A cross in memory of Father Nicolas Viel, in the Parc régional de l'Île-de-la-Visitation.

Designed by Buckminster Fuller, the American geodesic dome built for the 1967 World's Fair has become the first Canadian centre for environmental observation. It is now known as the Biosphère (page 49).

The city's first commercial street, de la Commune, looking from west to east up to the Bonsecours Market (extreme right) (pages 50-51).

The tourist artery of Old Montréal, old Saint-Paul Street, presided over by the Notre-Dame-de-Bonsecours steeple in the background (page 52).

A stunning example of residential renovation on Saint-Paul Street East (page 53).

One of many restaurants looking out on Place Jacques-Cartier (page 54).

Designed by architects Victor Bourgeau and Michel Laurent in 1861, these former warehouses belonging
to the Religious Hospitallers of Saint-Joseph have been transformed into the residential oasis of the Cours Le Royer.

The stately facade of the city's public library on Sherbrooke Street East
pays tribute to its architect, Eugène Payette (page 56).

The Beaux Arts style of the municipal court building (1912) contrasts
with the recently constructed Chaussegros-de-Léry building (right) (page 57).

Created by Philippe Hébert in 1895, the monument to Paul Chomedey, Sieur de Maisonneuve, the founder of Montréal, is framed by the two steeples of Notre-Dame Basilica, Tempérance and Persévérance (page 58).

The impressive choir of Notre-Dame Basilica. A crypt underneath the central aisle holds the remains of the former bishops of the metropolis.

The Bonsecours Market and Notre-Dame-de-Bonsecours
chapel on de la Commune Street East.

The stately columns of the Bank of Montreal
on Saint-Jacques Street.

Little Saint-Amable Street has become the preserve
of painters and portrait artists.

The culmination of Brother André's perseverance, St. Joseph's Oratory
is one of the city's religious shrines (page 62).

This statue, the work of George William Hill, dominates Dorchester Square in downtown Montréal.
It was erected in 1907 in memory of the soldiers who fought in the Boer War (page 63).

From the pinnacle of Notre-Dame-de-Bonsecours chapel, the statue of the Virgin protects arriving sailors (page 64).

Completed in 1914 by sculptor Alfred Laliberté, *La Fermière* lends her charms to the site
of the public market in the town of Maisonneuve, which was annexed to Montréal in 1918.

Completed in 1894 by architect Victor Bourgeau, the Cathedral Basilica of Mary
Queen of the World is a scale model of St. Peter's in Rome.

The doric pillars of the Ernest Cormier Building, seen from the old courthouse on Notre-Dame Street East (page 67).

On Sainte-Catherine Street, the transept of the former Saint-Jacques church
has been integrated into the Université du Québec à Montréal complex (page 68).

Built in 1705, the château of Governor Claude de Ramezay is one of the jewels of Montréal's patrimonial heritage.

On Drolet Street near Pine Avenue, the stairs of these row houses are all dressed alike in thick winter white (pages 70-71).

Montréal, a city of architecture

In Montréal, as in many of the largest cities of the world, architecture bears testimony to history. But in this city, architecture has played an unusually pivotal role in its development: we can even boldly state that architecture has actually been the source of its history. . . .

We need to go back to the year 1611 to find the starting point of this chapter, when Samuel de Champlain, as quoted by Father Charles-Honoré Laverdière, sighted *"quantité de prairies de très bonne terre grasse à potier, tant pour bricque que pour bastir"* ("many fields of lush potter's clay, suitable for both brick-making and construction"). As early as 1675, masons were active in Montréal, although wood was still the preferred construction material. From 1800 onward, brick was imported from Scotland, functioning conveniently as ballast during ship crossings.

But the most significant event affecting Montréal's architecture happened on July 8, 1851, when the most terrible fire ever swept through the city: 1,200 homes and buildings were burned to the ground. The Municipal Council prohibited any wood construction thereafter. From then on,

A harmonious blend of past and present: Christ Church Cathedral on Sainte-Catherine Street West silhouetted against the backdrop of the Place de la Cathédrale (page 72).

Three eras of Montréal architecture as seen from Phillips Square: Christ Church Cathedral, The Bay (formerly Morgan's) department store, and the Place de la Cathédrale.

architecture would impose its indelible mark on the city and shape the profile of Montréal.

Thus began the era of row houses. Land lots were broken down into narrower strips and contractors erected rows of houses, both typical and anonymous in style, which were then sold back through real estate promoters. At that point, the humble brick gained widespread acceptance: from being porous and round-edged, it became smooth-surfaced and multicoloured. On the other hand, cut stone was the trademark of posh mansions, and decorative facade elements — wrought-ironwork, festoons and cornices — were selected from catalogues and imported from the United States. Pieced together on site, they gave the buildings of this era a distinctive style.

About then, Montréal was dubbed "the city with a hundred steeples." At the same time, buildings dedicated to the service of various religious expressions were, without exception, relocated to the western area of the downtown core, on Sainte-Catherine Street (the Anglican Church's Christ Church Cathedral) and on Place du Canada (the Roman Catholic St. James the Elder Cathedral, more commonly called Mary Queen of the World Cathedral). The anglophone ruling class settled nearby in what became known as the Golden Square Mile, on the southern slope of Mount Royal, where they erected the kind of luxurious residences that you would expect of a social caste holding more than 70 percent of the whole country's wealth.

Around 1880, the more economical flat roof replaced the slanted roof, now that the necessary components — tar sheeting, flashings, drains and vents — were being produced in local factories. The typical extravagance of the times, or perhaps the fancy of Montrealers longing for a unique architectural style, led to the false mansard roof, which strongly emphasized the roof edges. Others added

The People's Bank Building, built in 1870 by architect Maurice Perrault, stands on the northeast corner of Place d'Armes.

to what were dormer windows, turrets and even bow windows. Balconies of wrought iron or turned wood and moulded doors were further evidence of the picturesque Victorian style.

A second wave altered local architecture around 1900, when changes to the land-registry survey plans permitted houses to be set back wherever back lanes were provided. From then on, stairways leading to upper floors were set in front, a feature typical of many streets in the city.

Commercial architecture, for its part, was not to be outdone. The advent of the elevator put an end to the five-storey restriction on buildings, stimulating the construction of skyscrapers, the first of which was completed on Place d'Armes in 1888. Municipal aldermen imposed, however, specific standards, such as incremental setbacks of higher floors from the building base. Such was the case with the Aldred Building on Place

d'Armes and the Sun Life Insurance Building next to what is now known as Dorchester Square. Started in 1913, by the time it was finally completed in 1933 the Sun Life Building was — at 26 stories — the tallest building in the British Commonwealth.

By the early fifties, Montréal had a new problem: it was literally choking, and drastic measures were needed. One solution: to widen Dorchester Boulevard (now René Lévesque Boulevard). Hundreds of buildings were demolished, opening the door to the commercial city of today. Designed by architect I. M. Pei, the cross-shaped

Section of the Queenston granite facade of the Customs House on McGill Street in Old Montréal.

building of Place Ville-Marie, completed in 1962, boldly straddled the railway tracks of Central Station and became the city's new trademark. Built at the same time, the 184-metre-high Canadian Imperial Bank of Commerce tower was the tallest in the world made entirely of prefabricated panels. The National Bank elected to buck the trend of building downtown, preferring to assert its presence in Old Montréal. It engaged architects David and Boulva to design its new headquarters on Place d'Armes in 1965. Since then, many buildings have been added to the city's landscape, but they still must meet the overall height restriction : none can exceed 230 metres — the height of Mount Royal.

Come along with us as we revisit these architectural testaments to the various periods of Montréal's history. Whether sumptuous or Spartan, they are all a part of the colourful mosaic of Montréal.

The image of the Casino de Montréal is graciously mirrored
on the still waters of Lac des Îles.

Dwarfing the Stock Exchange Tower (left), the building at 1000 de la Gauchetière Street West
is the tallest in the city (page 77).

A fresco of colours on Drolet Street
near Roy Street.

Elegantly detailed facades
on Saint-André Street.

A picturesque row of gables on
Saint-André Street south of Sherbrooke Street.

Stone masonry from the Victorian era adds to the charm of Square Saint-Louis, created in 1851.

The delightful side of the January 1998 ice storm, on Saint-André Street (page 81).

The silent aftermath of a snowstorm on Laval Street, facing Square Saint-Louis (page 82).

Wrought-iron balconies and stairways on Drolet Street, near Mont-Royal Avenue (page 83).

The unusual profile of the Habitat 67 residential complex completes the makeup
of Bickerdike Basin and the Iberville Passenger Terminal for cruise ships (right) (pages 84-85).

St. George's Anglican Church is surrounded by its imposing neighbours, among them the building
at 1250 René Lévesque Boulevard West (left) and the Laurentienne tower (behind).

Initiated in 1928 and completed June 3, 1943, the Art Deco structure
of the Université de Montréal is the masterpiece of architect Ernest Cormier.

Since its opening in 1912, the Ritz-Carlton Montréal hotel on
Sherbrooke Street has typified the luxury of the Golden Square Mile (page 88).

The cupola of the Cathedral Basilica of Mary Queen of the World
stands against the facade of the building at 1000 de la Gauchetière Street West.

Three giants from different eras: the Sun Life Building (left) yielded its title
to the Canadian Imperial Bank of Commerce building (right), then to the building
at 1000 de la Gauchetière Street West (background) (pages 90-91).

Adorned with a turret, this Victorian-style villa stands on Gouin Boulevard East at Papineau Avenue.

A stately mansion on Belvedere Road in Westmount.

Turrets enhance the Castle Apartments
on Sherbrooke Street West.

Row houses on Dorchester Boulevard
in Westmount.

Joined stairways on Saint-Hubert Street
near Rachel Street.

Garret windows and false mansard
roofs on Tupper Street
near Saint-Marc Street.

Turrets, bow windows and gables adorn
these row houses on Saint-Hubert Street
below Sherbrooke Street.

The site of the main events of the XXIst
Olympiad, the Olympic Stadium, as
seen from the western esplanade.

Shaughnessy House and the Canadian Centre for Architecture, an audacious
combination conceived by architects Phyllis Lambert and Peter Rose,
on René Lévesque Boulevard West.

The four towers of the Complexe Desjardins
from the plaza of Place des Arts.

Religion and finance in symbolic harmony
(page 101).

Montréal, a green city

Among North American cities, Montréal could very well hold the record in terms of greenery. More than half a million trees grace its streets, both adding beauty and helping curb pollution. And for more than a hundred and forty years, successive municipal administrations have pledged to the citizens to increase the amount of public green space, a promise which continues to be fulfilled.

Around 1850, the city was faced with a serious problem: both the Catholic and Protestant cemeteries located downtown had reached their capacity. At the same time, the metropolis was expanding in that very direction. Thus the city decided to purchase tracts of land on the northwestern slope of Mount Royal, and the cemeteries were relocated in 1853. Meanwhile, the upper classes began to settle on the southern slope of the mountain. In 1863, to curb this threat, a long-sighted city councillor named A. A. Stevenson proposed to turn the mountain into a public park, and a commission was formed to buy back properties from their various owners. Total costs exceeded a million dollars, but Montréal ended up with some 200 hectares (494 acres) of green space. The land was entrusted to the most qualified landscaping architect at the time — Frederick Law Olmstead.

Olmstead's fame had already been established with the completion of New York's splendid Central Park back in 1857. Taking into account the existing plant species and

A babbling brook on Île Sainte-Hélène contrasts with the hustle and bustle
of the city in the background (page 102).

The monument to Louis-Hippolyte Lafontaine,
at the south entrance of the park bearing his name.

land conditions, he advocated a network of roads and paths, the construction of a funicular elevator reaching the mountain summit, an observation chalet and a pond — the future Beaver Lake. The park was opened to the citizens on May 24, 1876, even before the project was completed.

Mount Royal Park would change with the years. An observation restaurant was built in 1906 and the elevator dismantled in 1919 for security reasons. In 1924, the Saint-Jean-Baptiste Society erected an illuminated cross, which soon became the lasting symbol of the city. Under pressure from citizens, the Montreal Tramways Company implemented, in 1930, a spectacular tramway line restoring access to the mountain summit. The following year, a new chalet was designed by architect Claude Beaugrand-Champagne. Among its charms for Montrealers was the possibility of attending concerts under the stars. As for Beaver Lake, it was completed in 1937. The tramway tracks' right-of-way was paved over in 1960 and became Camillien-Houde Way, in tribute to one of the most popular mayors of the city.

On a site formerly the property of James Logan but then rented from the federal government by the city, another green haven was added in 1889 — the remarkable Lafontaine Park. Beginning in 1900, a natural hollow on the site was converted into two ponds connected by a waterfall and spanned by a romantic bridge. The finishing touch came in 1929 with the addition of a magnificent illuminated fountain. That same year, the park became home to a zoo. In 1958, a stage was erected — le théâtre de Verdure — and the zoo was enlarged, becoming le jardin des Merveilles. (It closed in 1989.) Five monuments have been placed throughout the park, including one of Dollard des Ormeaux (1920) and one of Quebec bard Félix Leclerc (1990).

The seasonal charm of blooming apple trees
in Montréal's Botanical Garden.

A late but no less worthy entry, the immense Maisonneuve Park, previously the property of the town of Maisonneuve, was added to Montréal's inventory of green space in 1926. The park was eventually divided into three main areas: the magnificent Botanical Garden, laid out in 1936 by architect Frederick A. Todd and based on the recommendations of Brother Marie Victorin (Conrad Kirouac), a renowned naturalist and writer; the sports facilities area in 1957, including the Maisonneuve Sports Centre and Maurice Richard Arena; and finally, a golf course in 1923. The course was expanded from 9 to 18 holes in 1926, with another 18-hole course being added in 1966. When the 1976 Olympic Games were awarded to Montréal, new facilities were added — the Olympic Stadium, the Velodrome and the Athletes' Village. Let's also mention that Pôle Maisonneuve, as it is now referred to, is contiguous to the Cité-Jardin district, a project of the Union économique d'habitation launched in 1942 to mark the 300th anniversary of Montréal. The area's streets are lined with gloriously mature trees and — an original touch — each one is named after the species of tree planted along it.

The many regional parks scattered around the island's perimeter complete the city's green-space roster. Among those are the Parc régional de l'Île-de-la-Visitation, Saraguay Woods and the Parc régional du Cap-Saint-Jacques. Each park is accessible by public transit and crossed by clearly marked trails that invite restorative strolls and offer a chance to reconnect with nature. Finally, a network of dozens of kilometres of walking trails and linear parks, especially those along the Lachine Canal and the Rivière des Prairies, criss-cross the island.

The person anxious to get away from the frantic activity of the city is at no loss for alternatives. Montréal has maintained the charm of scores of avenues lined with century-old trees,

A restful pause near one of the numerous ponds
of Montréal's Botanical Garden.

perfect for quiet walks, while also preserving the fragile ecosystems surrounding the island. Without a doubt, Montréal deserves its reputation as a green city.

The Casino de Montréal, a jewel in its greenery case.

The downtown area as seen from the Lachine Canal embankment (page 107).

On the southern slopes of Mount Royal, a summer bandstand silhouetted against the cross-shaped Place Ville-Marie (pages 108-109).

The best-known symbol of Montréal,
the illuminated cross atop Mount Royal,
overlooks the imposing
Sir George-Étienne Cartier Monument.

Autumn brings its own gentle beauty
to one of the numerous pathways
in Mount Royal Park.

Pedestrians and cyclists share the linear
park along the Lachine Canal.

One of the many wooded areas of Montréal's Botanical Garden (page 112).

The environment is the common denominator between this tree
and the ecological centre behind it, the Biosphère on Île Sainte-Hélène.

A summer Sunday ritual: a tam-tam
happening on the eastern slope of
Mount Royal.

The lookout on Camillien-Houde Way.
The Protestant cemetery
is partly visible at right.

The belfry of the former Saint-Jacques Church, integrated with the buildings of the Université du Québec à Montréal, emerges from the canopy of trees gracing Saint-Denis Street (page 116).

Visual opposites: the greenery of Île Sainte-Hélène against the backdrop of downtown.

An autumn symphony in Lafontaine Park (pages 118-119).

Century-old trees on de Lorimier Avenue north
of Laurier Avenue (page 120).

A rainy autumn morning on Saint-Joseph Boulevard
at Saint-Hubert Street.

A thicket of Himalayan birches
in the Floralies Garden
on Île Notre-Dame.

An invitation for a stroll on
Mont-Royal Boulevard
in Outremont.

Montréal at dawn.

The Floralies Garden harbours many attractions,
among them this replica of typical first-century arches
and this patch of red salvia.

A pedestrian rest area on Île Sainte-Hélène.

A closeup of the graceful waterfall
under the bridge (at right).

Beaver Lake is visible
beyond this wooded area
atop Mount Royal.

The city at sunrise.

Montréal, a multiethnic and multicultural city

t is no accident that every year Montréal welcomes increasing numbers of visitors from every corner of the world. For decades now, Montréal has been known as a cosmopolitan and international city. Thirty-five languages are spoken here — not including dialects — and more than thirty religions are practised. This input from around the world has contributed to Montréal's reputation as a gastronomical Mecca: its more than 6,300 restaurants offer almost every culinary delight imaginable.

But how did this cross-breeding phenomenon start? Leaving aside the two founding nations and the Loyalist American influence that marked the end of the 18th century, the first international presence came with the massive Irish immigration. Driven by famine out of their native country, the Irish settled in Montréal from 1847 onward. Being strong and tireless labourers, most of them found work near their living quarters building the Victoria Bridge. Their total assimilation into the mainstream of Montréal life generated one-of-a-kind situations. For example, the Irish church on Centre Street in Pointe-Saint-Charles, St. Gabriel's, is no less impressive than its French neighbour, L'église Saint-Charles, the two churches sharing the same parish in total harmony. Furthermore, the Irish shamrock appears next to the French fleur-de-lys on the Montréal flag!

A vendor presents his selection of fresh produce at the Atwater Market, just as his predecessors have done since 1932 (page 130).

The pride of Little Italy, Casa Napoli Restaurant on Saint-Laurent Boulevard.

The Jewish presence in the city dates to 1768 when the first Sephardim arrived. But it was in 1881, when a large Ashkenazic contingent emigrated from Russia, that the Jewish community gained a foothold. Settling near Saint-Laurent Boulevard and on the cross-streets of the Mile-End district before relocating to the north slope of Mount Royal and the Côte-des-Neiges area, the newcomers lost no time in setting up a network of community establishments — schools, hospitals and social services. For their part, their fellow Montrealers quickly learned the meaning of words like "bagel" and "delicatessen," delectable additions to the local gastronomical vocabulary.

Italians came into the picture around the same time. Craftsmen from the north and rugged farmers from the south of Italy first settled in Piccola Italia near the harbour, and then near the Canadian Pacific Railway tracks in the northern part of the city, where they found maintenance work. By 1910, the size of the Italian-speaking community warranted the creation of an independent parish, Notre-Dame-della-Difesa, in the area thereafter known as Little Italy. The following year, Charles-Honoré Catelli established a pasta plant on the corner of de Bellechasse and Drolet streets. Its products soon found their way into every local cupboard. When, in 1931, the Place du Marché-du-nord (now known as the Jean-Talon Market) was developed as a Depression-era public-works project, it served as another way to bring the Italian and French communities together.

This well-known bakery is prized
by its patrons who come day and night
in search of their favourite bagels.

With the completion of the transcontinental railway in the West in 1885, many Cantonese workers who had helped to build it relocated to Montréal, at first finding jobs as launderers. Here, much like elsewhere, they formed their own district, a tiny enclave in the downtown area. In the twenties, the most prosperous used their savings to start restaurants and open grocery stories, adapting Oriental flavours to North American tastes. The end of the embargo on Chinese immigration in 1946, and especially the new Immigration Law of 1967, opened the doors to newcomers from all over Asia. The list of countries of origin of new Montrealers now included the Philippines, Korea, Vietnam, Taiwan and Hong Kong.

Although the Greek community had already been established in Montréal since 1850, it was mostly since 1950 that these hard-working labourers and businessmen first congregated on Park Avenue and then on Prince-Arthur and Duluth streets, which, thanks to them, have become busy pedestrian malls. Yesterday's dishwashers and waiters became today's entrepreneurs, and they now control some 70 percent of Montréal's restaurant empire. But their most prized contribution remains the *psarotavernas* and souvlaki spots, with their perennially festive atmosphere.

Montréal also became home to black immigrants from the United States, whose service as Red Caps (porters) was prized by railway companies. Montréal, which had already welcomed a large Caribbean community, started vibrating to the rhythms of black music. In 1928, Jamaican-born Rufus Nathaniel Rockhead opened the door of what was then Montréal's largest nightclub, Rockhead's Paradise, at the corner of Saint-Antoine and

Sushi is the featured dish
of this Mile-End Japanese restaurant
on Bernard Street.

Mountain streets, introducing Montrealers to the new sounds of jazz and rhythm and blues. Music lovers thrilled to the performances of Oscar Peterson, Billie Holiday, Ella Fitzgerald and, of course, Louis Armstrong.

A single word encompasses this fantastic blend of more than forty-five nations within one city — *wunderba*r !

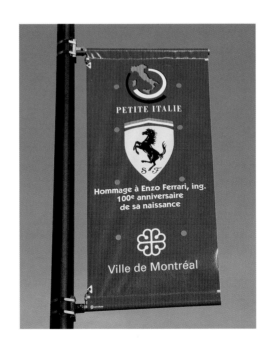

A municipal banner praises
one of Italy's favourite sons.

A group of regulars at Caffè Italia,
a rallying spot for Italian sportsmen on
Saint-Laurent Boulevard.

All Italian specialties can be found on this stretch
of Saint-Laurent Boulevard
near Jean-Talon Street (page 136).

Since its opening in 1931, Schwartz's restaurant
has been a favourite among
Montréal's gastronomes.

Autumn fare at the Atwater Market (page 138).

Who can resist the engaging smile
of this vendor at the Jean-Talon Market (page 139)?

Racial and social barriers give way to the beat of the tam-tams,
in the middle of the crowd (page 140) . . .
. . . or in the middle of the action!

Attractive open-air cafés flourish on Saint-Denis Street
in the Latin Quarter (page 142).

A Hasidic Jew strolls on Saint-Viateur Street (page 143).

Choosing is the only problem at the Jean-Talon Market, where prices are still quoted in imperial units (pages 144-145).

"May pleasures multiply in Chinatown"
declares this archway on Saint-Laurent Boulevard.

A bust of Dante overlooks the plaza
next to Notre-Dame-della-Difesa
Church in the heart of Little Italy.

The restaurants along the pedestrian
mall on de la Gauchetière Street
invite strollers to discover
the mysteries of Oriental gastronomy.

A portrait artist at work
on Saint-Vincent Street.

Buskers bring together all ethnic groups
on Place Jacques-Cartier.

Chinese shadows on
de la Gauchetière Street . . .

. . . and radiant colours at
the Jean-Talon Market.

An invitation to serenity:
the Chinese pavilion
at the Botanical Garden,
an original design
by Asian craftsmen.

Nighttime enchantment:
the festival of Chinese lanterns
at the Botanical Garden.

Shops catering
to the most exacting tastes
can be found
on Greene Avenue
in Westmount.

Summer is synonymous
with open-air Italian terraces
on Saint-Laurent Boulevard.

Montréal,
city of Montrealers

Within every Montrealer lies a dormant reveller and — could it possibly be a co-incidence? — it seems that Montréal is always staging major events sure to gratify instantly that insatiable appetite for entertainment.

Since its early days, Montréal has been a major player on the arts and entertainment scene. In 1825, brewer John Molson opened the Royal Theatre on the present site of the Bonsecours Market; it featured no less a personage than Charles Dickens in a major character role during his stay in Montréal in 1842. Next came the Shakespearean theatre of Moses Judah Hayes in 1847, and then the famed Monument National on Saint-Laurent Boulevard in 1893, where Elzéar Roy started the first theatre company —

Les Soirées de Famille (Family Evenings) — less than five years later. An-other significant date is, without question, Sep-tember 21, 1963, when Salle Wilfrid-Pelletier of Place des Arts was inau-gurated. With its 2,980 seats, it is still Montréal's premier venue for artistic events.

Fairs and exhibi-tions have always been popular with Montreal-ers. On August 23, 1860, before officially driving in the last rivet of the Vic-toria Bridge, the future King Edward VII inaugu-rated the magnificent Crystal Palace, a scaled-down replica of the fa-mous London exhibition

An attentive crowd enjoys a free concert during the
Montreal International Jazz Festival (page 156).

The thundering finale of a fireworks display at
La Ronde illuminates the profile of the Jacques Cartier Bridge.

site, erected at the corner of Peel and Sainte-Catherine streets. The majestic building with its elegant glass enclosures was later relocated to the foot of Mount Royal. An ill-fated fire destroyed it on July 30, 1896.

Montréal witnessed its first winter carnival in 1883, when a massive ice castle — complete with electric lights, if you please! — was set up on what is now Place du Canada. The carnival was so successful that in 1887, Place Jacques-Cartier was commandeered as a second site for the winter festivities. Revellers hurtling down the slides set up at its north end landed on the frozen St. Lawrence, almost four hundred metres from their starting point.

Music lovers had their turn in 1892, when a huge 5,800-seat auditorium was built at Sohmer Park, next to the Clock Tower Basin. A few kilometres east, the rides of Dominion Park started drawing crowds in 1905, to be later superseded by those of Belmont Park in 1923. Moviegoers were treated to the first movie house in North America, the Ouimetoscope, which opened January 1, 1906, at the corner of Sainte-Catherine and Montcalm streets.

Sports buffs have not been ignored and the stadium gods are countless, beginning with the Montréal Canadiens, who first took to the ice in 1909 and went on to become the most famous hockey team of all time. The spirits of Georges Vézina, Howie

Morenz and Maurice Richard still haunt the celebrated Forum on Sainte-Catherine Street, although games are now played at the Molson Centre. Montrealers have had a special place in their hearts for baseball ever since the famed Delorimier Stadium

The first event of the annual Tour de l'Île, when youngsters take over the city's streets.

opened its doors on May 5, 1928. Here, some 22,500 fans could attend games played by the Royals, a farm team of the Brooklyn Dodgers. And in this very stadium, the applause for the feats of Jackie Robinson, the first non-white player in major-league baseball, brought the house down. Memories of this era were rekindled forty years later at Jar-

ry Park, when the Montreal Expos joined the National League.

Montréal is also endowed with many museums — twenty-eight, in fact. The best known is probably the Montreal Museum of Fine Arts on Sherbrooke Street, built in 1912. Host to numerous acclaimed exhibitions, its collections are on a par with those of the McCord and Pointe-à-Callière museums, repositories of Montréal's historical heritage.

Where Montréal truly stands head and shoulders above other cities, however, is in its special events and the huge crowds they consistently attract. The Montreal International Jazz Festival began in 1980; the Benson & Hedges International fireworks competition was launched in 1985; the Just for Laughs Festival booted up in 1983; and the Francofolies de Montréal started lifting the roof in 1989. Each of these festivals draws more than a million people annually. And then there's the Tour de l'Île, the world's largest event of its kind, where every year some 45,000 bicycle riders tour a 65-km route along the streets of the city. Actually, and as unbelievable as it may sound, Montréal totals more days of scheduled activities than there are days in the year!

Add to the above the parades and shows held for special events or on anniversary dates, from St. Patrick's Day to Saint-Jean-Baptiste Day, and you can sympathize with the poor Montrealer faced with the decision of what to do for fun. And should the un-

Enjoying fresh air on Mount Royal
on a sparkling winter day.

imaginable happen peals — there is vised local gathering a public park. Mon- more than the ex- to congregate at one door cafés and wa- the city's main arter- you have to seek out you never have to time!

— that nothing ap- always an impro- or a performance in trealers need no cuse of a sunny day of the many out- tering holes lining ies. In Montréal, peace and quiet, but look far for a good

A typical crowd rallies at the end
of a traditional Saint-Jean-Baptiste Day parade.

Improvised shows rally the crowds
around the plaza of Place des Arts
during the Francofolies de Montréal.

Sainte-Catherine Street belongs
to the crowds on festival nights.
A terrace on Saint-Denis Street
near Mont-Royal Avenue.

Buskers are always popular,
whatever the hour,
on Place Jacques-Cartier.

A wild mix of neon lights
on Sainte-Catherine Street West.

The tower of the Olympic Stadium in the
background looms over the nightlife
of Mont-Royal Avenue.

A rendez-vous on
Saint-Denis Street (page 166) . . .

. . . where bistros and terraces
typical of the Latin Quarter
abound (page 167).

The impressive Pointe-à-Callière
Museum towers over the buildings
of Old Montréal (page 168).

Welcome to the Casino de Montréal!

The pillars of the Montreal Museum of Fine Arts
frame its new annex across
Sherbrooke Street West (page 170).

Place des Arts, Montréal's
premier venue for cultural events.

After the ice storm, on 1st Avenue
in the Rosemont neighbourhood.

Life gets back to normal between
the snowbanks on Duluth Street.

Skaters gather at Lafontaine Park across
from the central branch of
Montréal's public library.

Horse-drawn carriages are part of the family
atmosphere near the Mount Royal chalet.

The Fête des Neiges is the ideal opportunity
for short-lived ice castles . . .

. . . and for snow slides,
of course (page 177)!

Stairways on Saint-Hubert Street capture the eyes
of passersby riding their bikes . . .

. . . or on foot.

Even lanes have charms of their own,
like this one in the Rosemont neighbourhood (page 180).

The outdoor terraces on Place Jacques-Cartier
prove to be irresistible to strollers.

Crowds invade the Old Port during
the Just for Laughs Festival (page 182).

The end of a busy day for both drivers
and horses on de la Commune Street.

Motion and stillness meet
at the Berri-UQAM metro station.

Famous artists attract crowds during
the Montreal International Jazz Festival.

Saint-Laurent Boulevard — always
at the leading edge of cultural trends.

An improvised performance
on Place Jacques-Cartier.

The boutiques and bistros
of Crescent Street set the trends
for Montrealers.

Place Jacques-Cartier —
an invitation to relax.

The inclined tower of the Olympic Stadium
is the highest of its kind in the world (page 190).

The Molson Centre, the temple
of hockey aficionados in Montréal.

Montréal, the metropolis of Quebec

How can one sum up the countless attractions of Montréal? An endlessly animated city, forever fascinating, occasionally mysterious, sometimes peaceful and sometimes provocative . . . would it be right to say, as Quebec songwriter Jean-Pierre Ferland once wrote, that *"Montréal est une femme"* ("Montréal is a woman")?

Far from coveting megalopolis status, Montréal has opted to remain a city of human proportions, which accounts for its charm. Maybe this explains why the city has become a compulsory stop on the international-events circuit. Whether for prominent conventions or Formula 1 racing, Montréal is increasingly the obvious choice.

This well-earned reputation is not based on chance, for Montréal caters to all tastes, from the simplest to the most extravagant. And maybe on account of the unexplainable magnetism it exerts upon former residents and fascinated tourists alike, Montréal is a city that lures you back — whether for another stay . . . or forever.

For whatever the hour, the day or the season, Montréal is always the same and always different. From dawn to dusk, from the hot days of summer to the aftermath of winter blizzards, Montréal continues to replenish its store of pleasures.

This uncommon diversity likely explains

Montréal's answer to the Champs-Élysées —
McGill College Avenue from Place Ville-Marie (page 192).

The St. Lawrence River divides the downtown
core from the suburbs of the South Shore.

how Montréal has earned its coveted reputation as a hospitable city, whatever the season. Here, tourists can find luxurious lodging convenient for winter sports, or some friendly elbowing, whether at the Grand Prix du Canada or near the set of one of the many movies filmed in the city. They will notice that language barriers are quickly removed as friendly residents will swiftly resort to international sign language if needed, in typical Montréal fashion.

And when conversation runs out, Montréal speaks for itself, displaying its treasures for all to see. From the reflections on glass-enclosed buildings by day to the thousands of fireflies blinking in the apparent stillness of the night, Montréal never sleeps. Graciously, Montréal lets you gaze in wonder at the symphony of shapes and colours, at the interplay of dark and light, that generates not one but hundreds of images, unexpected and unforgettable.

For all these reasons — and many more, depending on the place and mood — Montréal truly deserves the coveted title of Quebec's metropolis. Whether you are a tourist or a long-time resident, you will always find another street, patch of greenery, boutique or show to add to the already large collection of sights in a city that, from one day to the next, is, and will never be, the same. . . .

The building at 1000 de la Gauchetière Street West
is downtown's highest.

Take a final look at Montréal and feast your eyes on some of its fabulous scenery, letting the impact of an unconventional perspective or unusual lighting sink into your consciousness. Who knows? Maybe this sampling of images will become the starting point of a wonderful adventure, piquing your curiosity and stimulating you to discover the innumerable visual delights of this city.

Montréal, the metropolis of Quebec, is calling you. So let yourself go!

A crowd favourite — racing driver Jacques Villeneuve
on the track named for his father.

The Stock Exchange Tower and the Royal Bank Building
soar above Old Montréal (page 196).

The north end of the city traces the horizon beyond
the dark shadow of the mountain, as seen from downtown.

An intense moment for Formula 1
driver Michael Schumacher.

The crowds attend preliminary
qualifications for the Grand Prix du
Canada at the Circuit Gilles Villeneuve.

Downtown at twilight.

Montréal ablaze as night falls.

The Maison des Coopérants,
Eaton Centre and Place Montréal Trust
line this stretch of de Maisonneuve
Boulevard.

The city's largest in 1878,
Windsor Hotel in the foreground
completes the perimeter
of Dorchester Square.

Erected on Île Sainte-Hélène, Alexandre Calder's *Stabile*
brings back memories of the 1967 World's Fair (page 204).

Near the entrance of the Banque Nationale de Paris,
La Foule illuminée is lighted from the inside at night.

A huge crowd at an outdoor concert on Sainte-Catherine Street
during the Montreal International Jazz Festival (pages 206-207).

Thousands of lights illuminate the downtown core at night.

Two challengers face off in the downtown arena: the building at
1250 René Lévesque Boulevard West
and the CIBC tower on the right (page 209).

An autumn sunset highlights
the brilliant colours of downtown.

The Sun Life Building with
Place Ville-Marie in the background,
from a southwest vantage point.

At the end of a perfect day,
Mount Royal Park is a favourite
for family outings.

With the Biodôme on its left,
the Olympic Stadium overshadows
the residential neighbourhoods east
of downtown.

The east end of the city
as seen from downtown.

Office buildings on René Lévesque Boulevard.

A tapestry of glass — the windows
of the Maison des Coopérants on
de Maisonneuve Boulevard.

The building at 1250 René Lévesque Boulevard and the CIBC
tower dominate the western area of the downtown core (page 216).

The open trench of the Ville-Marie Expressway burrows
under the Palais des Congrès in the background.

Completed in 1894 by architect Victor Bourgeau,
the Basilica Cathedral of Mary Queen of the World
is a scale model of St. Peter's in Rome (page 218).

The Queen Elizabeth Hotel and the Canadian National
building were built over Central Station,
one of the city's railway terminals.

Table of Contents

On a bright summer day, a view from above St. Joseph's Oratory
all the way to the peaks of the Montérégie region (page 220).

René Lévesque Boulevard digs a trench between office buildings,
looking east from Guy Street (pages 222-223).

Reflections at twilight (page 224).

Lithographed on Jenson 200 M paper
and printed in Canada at Interglobe Printing Inc.,
an affiliate of Transcontinental Printing Inc. in October 2000